Snail Mail Cursive

James Walton

Snail Mail Cursive

Snail Mail Cursive
ISBN 978 1 76109 465 1
Copyright © text James Walton 2023
Cover image: *Dream Home* by Susan Waddell

First published 2023 by
GINNINDERRA PRESS
PO Box 3461 Port Adelaide 5015
www.ginninderrapress.com.au

Contents

an absence of Giotto

in the damper sand
a streamer of seaweed
like an arrow at the bullseye

spirals

curled as it is
by a one-way wind
its mystery of being

perfect

the odds beyond reckoning
a circle for employment
its circumference deep enough

overt

until the tide reclaims
places beyond the living
of each day and night again

Blow your trumpet, Gabriel

(reprise)

The wind here peels skin
hones out the truth
birds stall in the veracity of physics

knowing the full irony
of a mad obligation

that long leap of colonial decades

leaving the river turned out
stench of mud howling condoms
dried out take aways

look to the south-west

where the clouds churn for hail
prepare to scrape calcium
make high cheekbones of panther

the unbroken gather there
an exhibition curated
by a jigsaw of lives

survivors of age and penury

and the small people
flecked at by society's tail
smile at what they can

one day a gentler hand
may arrange the pieces
patch the dreamy enamels

float the bottle into each House
rub the sides in new earnest
whisper a downpour of votes

if you stand into the gale
all it takes is breath

Cleaning the gutters, advent

each handful carries its own risks
from such fallow rusting
wandering ashes meant for sea
kidnapped by an idling wind,

the journey of leaves delayed
in the stalled gravity of autumn
beetle husks within dream
roof nails departing purpose,

desiccated chicks abandoned
concerto de Aranjuez
through an open window
forehead above to weatherboard,

debris falling to obeisance
sideways gusts push for witness
an awkward stance in weather
arms out and up a pelican,

of human clinging holding
to this chance of ballast
in a waning day's prolapse
spreadeagled for seasons,

the weight of each step down
loam alive beneath cuticles
a dust of primary evidence
out of survival's convenience,

the ladder eased a wingspan
this new station overhung
a light rain breathes ascent
everything released, anew.

Darebin Creek Crimes

Sometimes it was my turn
to buy the shilling's worth
of broken biscuits
from the new Summerhill shops

then the Ryans and me
would cut through the last paddock
for a watermelon
and the buckshot over our heads

broke up like comets
entering the atmosphere

we caught yabbies with the tin
and our crumbs we reckoned
floated all the way to China

decades later I ran into Johnny
at northlands car park

he killed that nice Buchanan kid
the lone cashier at the Drive In
with a sawn-off shottie
when he was fourteen

now he's just a tatt on Aids

but we had a laugh
I remember you all right Jimmy
how you brought down dragonflies

spitting out those stolen pips

your aim was that good
yeah but I only got community service
his toothless gums so wide

I could've been a dentist

Farewell by Sea

from hand to hand the burnished soil passes
cupped by palms conveyed in fist
to finally settle where dry throats breathe
and cake the slow bake of hearts here
held fast before the afternoon's conviction

we back into the wind to give you journey
the leather shoulder pieces clap
against head and neck and sky
below us the seals move as liquorice
in reveal to loll over the ancient basalt

I spill your urn finally to the daily whirl
watch as the Milky Way of you
flickers out through the untethered rip
drawn under the frolic of waves
to where the parallel choices fade

into this seethe of black hole edged
beneath the raging in constraint
of ashes burst tidal through memories
our lives collapsing for implosion
weighed down we lose our grasp on you

In the shop across from the Inverloch Library

On a table are house lots of photographs
and in them whole families that were somebody's
smiling or stern, loved or forlorn
can be reclaimed for twenty cents a time
bunned-up hair and broad-rim hats
looking away, or straight at Uncle Stan
the poses hesitant and a little awkward
as children fidget through a shutter
just as though, they're waiting to remember
where and how they know who you are.

Kilcunda, in the centre of October

the sun is saying summer
two mothers and toddlers
separated by exposed reef
shake a day's experience

one is reading Faulkner
the other Austen under shade

we're spread thin
as ducks holding on dawn
the membrane stretched
taut elastic pegged to places

how a body still wants flight

the trestle bridge is exposed
tide out as far as it goes
the bull kelp collapsed
all rolled dragon pieces

an old surfer ties up flippers
squints into his helloes and byes
he's had that dance with colours
where the water never lies

way out on the graphite
a fisher takes her chances

there is a lull of wave
you could be here tomorrow

like a note left in a pocket
gone through the washing

but the laughter comes in
deep down an undiscovered thing
where the lead runs smudging
writing, *but I want to live forever*

At the meter board

The power is off moonless night
stars broadcast, a lingua franca
in orbit of this fatal space.
Yet when dawn puts a finger
to my nose and the river speaks again,
everything is new innocent as arrival
without a shadow not as before.
Birds flutter through a reveille
small talk of waking things,
my life out on the perimeter.
The old world's a safety vest
too pithy, how the same instruments
cleaned and dressed made ornament.
A jangle of keys to witness chagrin
replacing fuses, where light has no mercy
only a well-honed opinion.

By a window, mid-fall

Sunday always has that gamey flavour
a secret tilt of baking dish, the table spoon
of flour. My arm in redoubt against a raiding fork,
the last of the potatoes, salty crisp top of mouth.
Toddlers falling off the soft chocolate of family,
lips fat with mutton, mashed peas for chins.
Mint by the gully trap in a mauve furze of hope,
turned sweet and sour alight in a crystal jug.
The shank bone boiled to briny float
somehow the first glimpse of fallow sea.

Daylight Saving, Eastern Standard Time

They told us cold milk was the blood of angels
it was during the Tokyo Olympics.
Our knees froze together in the morning
this was good discipline for us,
God knows there were people suffering.
And last night I cuffed the moon
tried to pull it down into the lounge,
a lever with a button dial an old typewriter key;
the one pinball machine in the corner shop
awkwardly sited, so your bum was pressed
up against the ice cream cabinet.

This morning at 3.33 the logging trucks
began their inexorable mathematics
unchallenged by the forward hour,
of the lost Third Theory of Relativity.
At 4.33 fully loaded in return
they pass each other one empty one full,
drop the high beam of simultaneous equation.
Four into sixty minutes the pod surfacing,
and all day the narwhal song of slowing –
for the curves as the air brakes hiss and moan
into the mechanics of physical impasse.

The dry road is a rage of cosmic dust;
it is never returned that hour multiplying each day
out of your reach when the clock is turned back,
a stammer lurks behind the pendulum.
The Guff full past reckoning as the rings of Saturn
clasp in acolyte formation waiting for the knock.
Now the years circle in a pack, nappies become Degrees;
who dares to raise the innocent sacrifice
shout out we can progress no more?
Beyond the incessant rapping someone is singing
'Will You Still Love Me Tomorrow'.

Do whales think in blue

Then I touched the wetted skin
fletching thoughts
the pod's skittish deference
a line of sight

If I'd said I loved you
there where ancient sands
kissed at my toes
like keys through ribbon to paper

Or the taste of shortbread
a slow melt of lemon myrtle
old mills in renovation
a scalloped turn of edges

We pushed the clumsy calf
shoving with our backs
until the sea opened its palms
in sudden rolling eptitude

There was nothing left to be
our feet squeaked on the beach
laughing with our sonar code
we shook hands with the sun.

from the north hide

the black swan soothes a promenade
bills through a pennon of underwing
a swamp harrier dallies in pirouette

as echidnas scowl their annoyance

a dauntless of pardalotes
whizzes to my ear

my season's first tiger snake
alive to water sways a ripple
frogs all bassy spruce

echo themselves

a rebound of spring sky
laughs back at a sprawl of sedge
where a frame of sleek water
breaks by a fatal leap

a smile of grey herons cast lives
out of this growing warmth

the wagtails and wrens weightlessly
jeté à jeté on the floating bank

the arcade oil by tea trees
lets go the thrush's call back
to a place I cannot bring focus

flousing the curve

I am turning left more
in the rectangular seduction of streets
on the dunes grass trees
all knobbly persistence shake a cautionary
the belief of footpaths
shallow by cracks in their secular metres
prise at sanctuary
solar streetlights linger abandon to day
fother to a wane
a diagonal gesture a shadow of curtsey
all theories in discount
a beshrew of galahs saunters knowledge
their slow arc of parodos
lets shine the declining setting onus
spreads my bending ways

Full English Breakfast

I will admit I'd like to have hair like Jennifer Aniston
from that show years ago something so luxurious and wild
starlings could gobble in and out of it lost toys might
occasionally reboot you know the plastic confederate
soldier his pedestal missing and a yo-yo done in doing
the walking the dog when some kid who was supposed
to be a friend stuck his foot out and your knees got grazed
and bloody and the whoop whoop of a surfacing submarine

or that curly dirty snow avalanche of the guy from Queen
the one who's still alive a straggle grand as an old mop
dragged through the wringers on a rusty metal bucket
you know that flick and look over the shoulder arrogance
of never ceasing growth a kind of capitalism by follicle
larger than the GDP of several nations washed by
an Olympic-sized pool of shampoo where a friend's lost
rescue cat meows out all slick and unhappy with the shine

not to have to look down in the morning at the comb over
on my toes as I tumble like an unwrapping mummy
from the too small shower coffin cubicle to carefully
brush my capriccio for breakfast where the hotel restaurant
tables are spilling over with a tsunami of well-dressed suits
thinking how the combined bounty of my shoulders
nose and ears might give Jen a run for her money when I hear
I don't speak Mandarin but you can have
the Full English Breakfast

Heart Stone

The cemetery cat asleep on the warm headstone
careless of the worthy mason's curfew

ignores the adjustment to place
my fingernails caught in the fierce scree of memory

I try to place the language of a pebble
from when we slept huddled at Roaring Meg
waking laughing snoring back at snowflakes

carried by a pilgrim's wanderlust
its granule beat beyond a relic's blessing

there is a continent between us
they are strangers, your family, after our time

even now do they know about your toe rings?
those keepsakes of the Kush market

a lonely chorus hum slips through forearm hair
the release of doves falters songs escape
an evening bids by light too short

this redeemed concession out of was
now a stranger's lilt toward recovery

a best suit shrouds over like a shag of wet ravens
graphite slow motion by crease endowed

you wanted to be buried a Viking

but here we are among the kindling
still held apart between oft trodden roads

Shall I introduce this parting remnant
fill in the song lines of your mystery
leave it to resonate by the sun translated?

Hero of the Soviet Union, Twice

Alexie Leonov's (30 May 1934–11 October 2019) Walk in Space, First

A tether of sixteen feet
is the degree of separation
between the escaping ink of forever
here, walking over the Volga's profile

etched out of a far Gulag
where my father Arkhip
us of Siberian birth
saw the commissars take him

an enemy of the people

like his son, dreaming of circumferences
the hatch too small
without the release of conscience
the sun too bright an enigma

five hundred kilometres out
Pavel knocking a spanner's message
to shrink by valve released
those first steps over Crimea

weightless before all accusation

to return within a capsule
painted as it was by forest fire

grim as a cell's silence

my family's boots all lit up

such small small steps
for a cosmonaut
nothing below or above
as the ash settled

about our release

Hideout, reprise

When death called uninvited
I remembered
buried outlaw long necks of beer

as tubers

under the deign of hydrangeas
splashing irises
beside the straggling hibiscus

a fallen rainbow

abeyance in rain
the returning blue chequer
a flap in the tree house

cornflowers adrift

ripcords

House H(a)unting, Fish Creek Victorian

An unborn dreaming hunger touched my wrist
outside the Nine Acres Café counting cars
as the southerly broke into fragments
the barista's earnest feathered design
I'm thinking of how you plaited the ingot beads
and bound up the kneaded lot
over your shoulder like a Scandinavian sweetbread

a triage of green years passed to me
ears of wheat not hardened by the sun
friable in the way new things breathe
and out of the silken parcels of listening
sounds only baying dogs can hear
the best choices that could not be made

never meaning to just a pure accident
the football landed on my cousin's head
knocking her down in the driveway
my uncle drove me three hours home
explaining good and evil and values
and did I see that rabbit rush over the road
I lied and said yes so as not be in the dark alone

out of the ancient songs of grass
a convocation of elemental striving
the first letter the final stroke the last wish
a Sunday morning newscast death
first encounter of wildfire incidents
the taste of hazelnut on a baby's crown

realising it would be too busy
crossing them off in lots of five
why come so much further east unwise
to another soggy falling down veranda
vagrant regrets on their knees reciting Marys
the Friday night make it right post
pass over prayers to make good their rosaried week

during the war my mother collected Yankee dollars
in a pony tail poised as a question mark
where the worn jaw line of Luna Park closed mid laugh
an old pier stretched out across quiet sighs in waiting
a silent point in mid horizon a cat on a window sill
above born-again jets sprung from coin in the slot

a gas heater's cracked honeycomb teeth
breathes out the smelly cooking hum
of the Victorian pressed metal ceilings
old empire colours gaudy and dour
along the hall the iron painted white
when someone got their Irish up
but by some grace left the intricate pattern tiles

a mohair scarf drapes across reupholstered chairs
catches what beams between hand sewn coverings
and the tiny threads of everything there is
shine their small diorama floating and settling
muffling the speed of light to a rundown torch
enough to outline how our limbs are formed no matter what

my life began in two small rooms a city away
wandering its slow punted canals
dodging school for rank creek and wild fennel
in boots of remnant polio
off landing me in a desiccate late autumn day
waiting for the break
absently rubbing where the iron still hurts a little

I missed the passing of Galway Kinnell

that bus went by as I fumbled for the timetable
through pockets full of things, notes for shopping,
a fob watch gift, flapping fabrics to weave

for I would have liked to reach your overlook
the salt scaped bench where 'Romeo loves Juliet'
and 'Tithonus was here' mark out our differences

final clues traced beneath the torn off piece
the sublime folly of being on time (always)
such scratchy irritation in a loose eyelash pause

we could have sat there watched arm in arm
ocean-grazing kelp and unreefed granite crops
while the deep polished obsidian of your voice

its carats saved so many souls from themselves
and this unkempt cliff point in danger of collapse
becomes the softest landing a feather's intersect

I begin to wonder

what may be said
of all the books, LPs, CDs
eclectic would be polite
a bohemian twist perhaps
the turntables,
speakers, amps, cassette decks
the 60s headphones
a stage of collection
which surprised even me
a too partial detritus and flotsam
the three Italian fine wool business suits
leftovers of negotiation
now dusty on the shoulders
those super-size knitted jumpers
several flocks to the wise
the silver Paris vest watch
a decades ago lover never took back
uninscribed in its beauty
the kids reports and hand paintings
they grew up while I was thinking
of ways to slow the falling eclipse
how she will deal with this
in her organised way
free of my chaotic architecture
tools bursting the garage and cupboards

the tally of life before and after
these whittled years now appropriated
I've left the will of everything
she can decide what to do
plant me to a tree or wild flowers
flesh or ash we return to the humus
top dressing for this restless orb

I play the perfect cover drive

Easing on to my back foot
Saturday early early summer, elevenish
a sound of cork like popping
the axe fall of linseeded willow
throughout the mowing suburbs

My spine straight as a lithe picket
Plane trees shady stalled on shutter
a mottled reminisce of Cazneaux
our border/kelpie Sophie
trotting back the drooly ball

Her jet coat a reel
in stoppled light from Van Gogh's head
a thwack in the fence holding on
the still of tactile breeze
my children, Shot, wanker,

can we have lunch

In Respite, at Sixty-six

I no longer seek to understand
the shilly shag of aspiration
more the settled stone
why try to steal the wind?

having seen the veils of rhetoric
fall to tumbleweeds
out of the ribs of ambition
skilled out slim as fishbone

swallow a broken habit breathe it out cloud
a thing of loose direction
consider the driveway
a persistence of grasses

a child asked me do the trees hold up the sky?
they must because they're higher
all purpose centre fold

life rails against the palings
or winds by a course of events
made firm as lighthouse standings
in the words of cast nets

this battery limited by mortal fatigue
as the flaw in an infant's summer
endless in its grasp will finally falter
at a rendezvous beyond all appraisal

Inverloch – Cape Paterson Road, late August

The car park at Eagle's Nest is nearly empty
and down the steep staircase, neatly arriving people
trickle in hesitation of a complete view.
A full tide has spread spongy wilted sand
all soft without reflection, a copse of twisted wattle
holds to purpose where the erosion bites.
Warning Signs don't stop visitors from testing
the Strait's gritty pull, the sea's hypnotic stride
tap dancing away on the buckle bright shoreline.
Kelp is wedged up at each end of the bay
a russet parenthesis in need of expression;
idling cormorants glide by
in their defiant bobbing coiffure.
A winter moon is stitched on a light denim sky
prescient in daytime, some Iranian children
laugh out Hello Mister chasing their runaway kite.
Beyond the craggy hide the Cape bends
in reverse crescent eyebrows over an ocean face,
cars make a way as greying follicles of squint
into the receding west.

Jesus They Must Think I'm Dead

we should do something about pain management
my doctor Eileen concerned my talon hands
what was my good knee
and the dull ache in my back need

My Body is a Temple OK?

pressing the green pensioner button
Old Bill comes in the reception door
moves slowly a square rule on a cane
across and out the waiting room slider

a horizontal elephant walk memory
through what was once his house
towards the pie shop
he knows won't last forever

in this town cars stop for pedestrians
the surfers have coffee under the parasols
of the world's most expensive health food shop
at Jill's bakery winner of the best on earth

flocks of gully tourists squabble to grab
of what Paris nodded the winning fare
in the library I see two of my collections are out
Jesus They Must Think I'm Dead

Bill's on the bench by the flagpole
making the chicken and vegetable shell
go a marathon in his mouth

the pastry light as heavens rising

he makes the cursory offer of crust
plated on what I see is the back cover
of my special edition the blurb obscured
politely I decline smiling for a biro

My Body is a Temple OK!

Jazz Festival Inverloch

Labour Day Weekend

Days flip verso
a large bass floating,
scored over the inlet breeze
pianists compete for what's left of cool.
Notes are transfused eternal,
the flamenco trio has a new language
George Michael to a different beat.
The sky draws sail boards in bluesy clefs
the old blokes banter in sets,
so familiar they change key with a look
marry Rodrigo in 'Autumn Leaves',
tapping feet counting in vintages.
Torch singers coy the crowd,
drummers get their solos
saxophones blow a curing mist.
Buskers play kiss chasey for a place,
strangers smile a harmony.
A day is gifted on to another
all silky wrapping smooth as sway.

Late Winter Sunday Reflection

Three houses down
on a morning with snow
I notice while out walking
a kangaroo in the vacant block
where they tore down the last
of the fishing shacks
to build three huddled units

She stands at full height to query
as I take a phone shot to prove
my presence in her moment

And how I wish to hold her
paw in hand with trust
back down the road to the Reserve
close the gate on this suburb
watch her hop and turn a farewell
float the gravity of leap

Wave a palm so close to mine
We could be family

She knows the truth with humans
the hurling want to be
waits for me to pass
delves deep into the long jump
better to leave that flowing symmetry
of tempting feed and boundary

One Easter at another place
marsupial arms reached by the sliding door
hungrily taking hot cross buns
from my children giggling giddy

On entering our lounge I stop to ponder
Can we ever be sure we've not met before?

Mallacoota guesthouse, between States

We slept in Henry Lawson's bed
*in the days when the world was wide**
at a place where pelicans and kangaroos
gambolled on a horizon of lawn
sloping to the inlet jetty
all those years ago
the road to Conran closed by forbidding rains
You ate shortbreads telling me the crumbs
could never forget us
the way they disappeared in the sheets
like fish diving to or away from bait
a forever slight of need
At smuggler's cove we rescued a penguin
the one station copper laughed
telling us to put it back there
giving us bandaids for our fingers
A long stretch of days bent our way
the veranda smell of ozone and bracken
pipe and shirt sleeves held up with elastic guards
the owner trying to find a place in the world
a Checkpoint Charlie the eye of the needle
You went through without me
just as I looked down to validate our passes

* The title of a Henry Lawson poetry collection

Leonard Cohen and the delayed Block Print drops in

I received a letter today 'To The Householder' on the address
in an envelope from Kingdom Hall of Jehovah's Witnesses
six stamps, from overseas, inside it was a photocopy
quoting Matthew 6: (9) (10) Jesus explaining
a bright hope for the future plus some bonus Isaiah
with a QR Code to the latest magazine my initials .org
a paperclip caught my nail in a gentle tag, Indian ink blurred
a different original hand spidery in its detail:

'You can only draw breath in winter, baby, the charcoal
in our making released, my thumbs now too full of pain
to hold the sacred butterfly. The way it filtered the sketch
when we tried to teach the law, the gentle tease of knowing
how seasons reproach the old, here, make of this plainsong
the unfinished things our bareknuckle youth, baby, how
living was the dying where I kissed your warm feet only
the sky our roof in Temple as all heavens tossed for worship.

(I send this on to you stranger, just in case you can appreciate
that my loss was only material, better than a bottle, all things
considered, although I have a faith in oceans, being as I am

Yours respectfully L.C.)'

Levee to Absence

the cards are brief this year
in shallow condolence
a levee to absence, broken

the scattered sorrow
left for salvage
how they talk of passing

yet visit as though gentle as
the first faint call
the quiet summons to duty,

steadfast the whether of breaks
the happiest dispersed

days drag through cement
mercury for the veins of us
caught in winter, November

veers without season
too cold for painting
this colour we were

a dash to break a sentence
run for cover, highlight
crimson for specifics

an outline to bridge
this stalling year's account

supernumerary to how and why
between twig and wake
this inconvenient bird

a rustle of dark, nests
then stirs unbeckoned
daubed as it must be

wily and propped against
a door of feathers for words
open notebook of hours

I sit the post waiting
sandbagging against breach

Marble

There's a cat's eye in my hand,
it changes colour with a spin
and sends out a different aspect each time.
Rolled on the grass refracting all angles within itself,
absorbing and emitting light
that's crossed centuries of lives.
Other fingers have dollied it,
pondered the aggregate in the middle,
how the black, red, and blue create green and yellow
inset a fall.
Someone had it before me and before them;
lost it for another to discover.
All around this big cerulean marble,
hands have closed over this captured rainbow
of continents merged in thought
and wondered at the turn.

Modern love tales

I'll put on *After the Gold Rush*, *Sgt Peppers, Blue*
how much a graph of me this gives
is best left for speculation

But I can tell you it's no different to fifteen
in a way, hold on to this avocado of a heart
wait for the slower beat

I can't make promises about days
because decades submerged by nature's balance
are a hidden rip in resurgence

That still water, here's my hand waving
always at my best with the light behind

There's a chance of rain
the way sense trawls a ripple
divining the way in or out

This fraught peace, all things being considered
flotation of a gentle principle
some of my recordings have the bends
elliptic on now band less turntables
while each replay travels on echo forever

Mine is just dentistry, thus I can pray for my oldest friend

I lack the faith of doorknobs or roads
the steadfast purity in purpose
an exhibit of solid testimony
between before during now and after
how hands or rain or dust cannot shake
the utility of being so

no minor inconvenience for direction
no reason to look beyond or under
but then doubt is a quiet virtue
applied as it is to wax over an incisor
to blunt a broken molar at the tongue
to pace the slow words

thus I can pray for my oldest friend
while the aloof surgeon intercedes
to halt the spread of decades
this wily thing remorselessly pacing
our born shadow gift and terror
mine is just dentistry

a contiguous shallow emergency
for the same day as your anaesthesia
maybe I can ask for something else, gas?
journey together to a dreamy theism
take hold of our retiring years
palm to brass handle, knee to bitumen

My life as a suitcase

you know before it happens
that malignant sock sticking out
giving the tongue to any onlooker
the handle grip looser than it was
no longer in control   as if we ever are

for years it flew at you sleepless
open and grinning swallowing the lot
no separation of the clean or used
a whale to your subconscious krill
the events tumbling in   losing magnetism

still my heart is going going
a bird caught in a room of mirrors
it will slow to a puff within a cheek
a lanteen opportunity of reflection
in felucca slow rescue   to follow markers

each piece where the current
takes its slow swab of your being
rounds up the loose stray events
sits on the bulging aspirant lid
writes the prescription of how to pack   by an unknown hand

not so recalcitrant reader returns to Pride and Prejudice

Jane, I remain Yours, &c.

My dear Lizzy if I may still be so bold
after 51 years of absence from Longbourn
exactitude being a virtue amongst friends,
as it is to be precise as it is to be worthy
can I speak of that struggle so contained
by society's rigours of want for decorum?
Be assured I delight in the fortunes
of the other Miss Bennetts outright
(thinking on a theme not so preordained),
as lapsing before your father's library fire
Lady Catherine's prying critiques indignant
her privilege speaks of my lucky entailment.
Fifteen years in the cast from First Impressions
two sets of heroine and hero misaligned
here the rub against class- station- honour,
appraised in reproach by gentle humour
its perspicacious truth has no slake of hold
although of this you may find slight amusement,
Darcy rising Adonis from Pemberley lake
(I wonder though did you imagine)!
such common faults in modern rumour.

Light here recedes from examination Elizabeth
I will take my leave as I must and allow
the family to reoccupy these pages of rooms,
your intrepid rummage over paddocks
has left me a little exhausted in contemplation
bested in each life's cautionary intermission.
Words mark and weigh up our journeys
the author's recant in search of that self
untrammelled the byways into Derbyshire.

Old joke in a sunny spot, yesterday

At the corner of Princes
and Cemetery Parade East
where Lygon Street leaves the shops
and tries to become a suburb
a billboard hangs off the iron balustrades
announcing Exclusive Grave Sites
Going Fast Enquire Now

(you might have to slow to see it)

it's one of those days
when the sun is as gentle
as lips on your forehead
and I have to laugh out loud
here as the mad traffic hurtles by
the bus horn detonates a moment
just enough to save a jay walker

(at the sign, not the jay walker)

whose earphones want to make that call
the fates almost colliding in pathos
an Ethiopian guy from the estate
hanging on amidst the private developments
smiles at me a rueful headshake
and I shouldn't (I know) but it happened
Yeah, they're dying to get in there

Nobody reads poetry any more,
Unanswered Prayers

wind whispers hurt
entreating new cold earth,
you should have stayed
a secret azure from afar

the alloy of eyes tempered
over this shrouded continent,
soot to the arteries
of coal mired government

smoke, is written under skin

there is no birdsong
but for this dry retch of trees,
still these ten hours of rain
unchained as rust now quietly clear

murmurs of fonts beyond dream
opening to christen the taste of sky,
this chance to hold out again
one primary state bold as genesis

Not so still life Winter un Blues

the jonquils are finishing and starting
a July day clear as a schoolyard bell
stellar heads brighter than chortle
look one way then the other
waiting to cross the tepid morning
of warm tendencies left out to dry
here the salty ice bites into tarragon
a bronzed memory of autumn rising
the oxalis periscopes at dive
weeded spheres in planetary align
laid on gravel the invasive memory
reaches for more fertile ground
a half sleep ginger cat resiles slowly
sniffs at chimney smoke aromatics
a pair of gloves loosed of form
wait patiently pillows in adjourn

Place in a Landscape

Another shirt ruined
the new calf breathing with me
ear to heart
my head on the tree fern curve
each of us too tired to rise
the gully folded about us
sliding down the steepness
to the road's bend
over to the yards
her mother calling
a mouth finds my finger
searching for milk
eyes wide between
fear and comfort
sepia beyond words
she lets me hold her face
this world slips into gear
resting on the back veranda
arms round my knees
in a hello
the king parrots hang upside down
a shelf of splashed paints
fall to pick the ground
my toes disappointing seeds.

Open pages, by the numbers

someone said
poetry is sky writing for the blind*

my curvature a broken horizon
bundled marionette
the rheumy strings entangled
for hope to unravel

having outlived
most who have been
corrected by a life span

thoughts drawn to the neon of fireflies

whoever it was
knew the ecstasy of reach
the anatomy of Icarus

the downfall of angels
a condensation point of reference

* A segment of a line from the poem 'Bequest' by Philip Martin

Poor Man's Chicken

Of a mountain
you are a footfall echo
the goat's enquiry

for the definition of ice

loose change spent
there is no news of spring
in this we are assuaged

no reconnaissance wings by

taste the butter and pepper
now here is a final crust
fresher than birth

splinters in toes

from a porch of strangers
a circle of amanuenses
to record the shorter straw.

Potato Classes

Spudders we were called
hill clay rabbits dirt tumblers
Aunt Astrid sewed and threw,

a 40-kilo bag of Dutch Creams
when eight months (and a half) pregnant
winning the picker and packer prize,

our cousin Tomasz always
had those girl catching moves
inherited in the womb,

a saucy swing of hip
an entice of shoulder shrug
and a smile so big as round the bay,

he could always find a room
in the difference between
Toolangi Delight or Russet Nooksack.

Ragnarök in the Coles supermarket car park

I found Jesus

in the kitchen, late
helping himself
to the sour dough loaf
some roast beef, mustard
I thought I'd take the chance
my lower back – a small miracle
but he only had advice, gentle exercise
back stretches. The Holy Ghost was hanging
literally, from the saucepan hooks
I'd expected a big irradiating dove
dropped to the bench top an Indian mynah
yellow beak Long John Silver hop
streaky feathers making a mess
nesting on the small coil
I couldn't boil an egg,
and asked them to leave.
When I saw them again
they'd been joined by an angel
busking outside the Centrelink office
at least the winged giant played well
but the scowl of superiority wasn't helping
next day, a broken guitar D string
motley ragged down and a vegan condom
marked their spot. A few weeks later

on the evening news, arrested for ram busting
a jeweller's window the 'Trinity Gang'
looked haggard and smug handcuffed together
to the remand centre, which caught fire
mysteriously. The graffiti on Spencer Street
big letters ASCENSION OK was in a colour,
that couldn't be identified.

My lumbar is better.

Renaissance, man, yeah

Friends rang to tell me
that Jim the elder had died
a man who always walked
as though still on the tractor
Hands bent wrought iron
escaped from an anvil
a frame always stooped
in pulling ragwort and thistle
at the bull's roar of eighty-nine
And that they were pregnant
in a mix of Estonia and Queensland
settled on my old place
where Dicksonia Antarctica
grow tall as dreams

Placing the rectangle of phone down
I took the bronzy old school bell
once used to call the children in
from the intrigue of paddocks
Twirling arms out and up
beneath an ornamental Manchurian pear
grizzly with late autumn mottle
ringing out the mowers blowers
chains saws and traffic
next door's rooster finally silent
jumping the fence away down the lane

Loud in the day as a drought breaking
and it did
the decibels bringing down a sky
months of rain lightning thunder
forking tossing bellowing change

Playing that wild alarm of joy
tolling its universal tongue
like the whole world needed it

rising Lazarus

things cannot settle
side cars clip
in a dead-end alley

suck the dough
off a sixpence
teeth around a chrysalis

moon inks a night
arabica on the x-ray

pull back the curtains
Bogong moths
knock away from rain

searching the latitude
of anchorage
by this safe harbour

Royal Icing, a Christmas Ditty

It was the silverfish
in the end
that finished
the highwayman's treasure

a malfeased piece
of Victoria's wedding cake
a sliver of majesty
kept wrapped

in muslin cloth
scissored from a pillow's hood
transported to Hobart in '49
absconding the famine of Dublin nights

and four months
at captive sea
handed down with the story
a simmering rebellion

taken out of the mouths
of noble gantries
along with seven shillings
and a pound of meat

secrets passed its way
until compounded and forgotten
to finally feed the worthy
in a Richmond pantry.

S.O.S

We send you our finest
though our words come
in hundreds of languages
there is only one instrument
used by all our peoples,

we are killing ourselves
over the different edges
of colloquial dissent
and versions of higher idioms
from the same mouths,

translate for us of how
flower buds and babies
reach for milk in the same way
as tongues await the deft drumming
of a sun's agency of new days,

come from beyond your stellar dialect
remind us that a kiss
is the most intimate grace of sex
that all tears taste of salt
and there is hope for us yet.

Salt and Vinegar Please

Some things aren't a colour
but more like that misty fetish
when you peel a mandarine,
and a fog from Rumi's pool
takes a moment out of the air.

The world is stalled on an errand
by a rindy beguile of wobble
a then coming back forever,
webbed over and through
a honeycomb lacquered with it.

Leaving you espaliered on a smile
warm bricks against your back
out front the crisp ironed world,
has winter in a laminate
as perfect as the first hot chip.

Your scalded tongue
mouthing more.

The Scarecrow

I could tell you of the hard hail of sixpences
on this speckly jumper with its barbed wire holes
and the elbow gash from knowing's use
where the mousing cat snoozles in,
or the sudden whack to the face
the first-time words stub into you from love's slammed door,
a teenage death before experience cures.

But there's a black cockatoo on a drawn branch
one eye primed ready to launch if I move,
a jerky breeze would be the dissolution of me.

I could sing you of the soft rime of an artichoke's glory
wrapping the curate's tonsure in unexpected daze,
where below the unspeaking tongue of my leathers
the cut down stalk shouts out with new emphasis
biding a season in just two steps away.

How love has no redemption date or return to sender
no use by in a business envelope without address,
the withdrawal notice pinned within these vestments.

That wind and wing have the measure of the duty in us all
taking the hat with loosed sunglasses,
the stuffing falls through the stake goes over
pantalooned chickens fossick the seeds of my charge here.
And way down, in the remnant of a fraying cyan sweater
pushy prickly leaves will weave their rise once more.

Scenes of the Rural Domestic

They go off like a sherbet bomb
settling joy all around
a new baby introduced at home
lickable as fairy floss in a swaddle

Great grandma is in the blue gin
telling of how he never worked a day
but she gave up the circus life
its elegant parabola of trapeze

Two cousins roll their own
in the symmetry of twins in a mirror
sweaters over folded arms
to disguise the handcuffs beneath

The screen doors are hanging on
as children bang in and out
running through everyone's place
jumping the dogs' sleepily drooling patience

Looking into eyes
that don't yet know their colour
a fart gurgles down my forearm
a smile an arching back

The smell of cooked chips
gets into everything
and you know absolutely
you know with absolute conviction

caught uncompromised in this cleft of living

that you would sever any ground
deny all causes or beings
to keep her safe here
from each and every predator

Sixty-eights

I have this garden about my head
where upturned things are set to rights
birds fly in and out
dropping twigs dropping droppings
there's a guitar with an elk fern propped
strings hang loose rusty for promise
the possum I buried has sprung to fig
a Moreton Bay the next owners can worry
the blue tongues are endlessly at it
not minding my step over tripsy
another piece of Irish strawberry tree
has crashed through the wood shed
the kikuyu has escaped recalcitrant
no end of round up can diminish it
the lemon tree sarcastically fruits all year
a swathe of plums won't confess to genus
wings beset everything
you're frustrated by my meandering
'Jim another fucking book is in the post
where's it going to go, at least read it.'
Ah, but where's it been Love
as a kookaburra snaps my glasses
I'll get to everything, eventually

Sixty-seven, 67, I recognise spectrum, again

in ankle-deep courage
seven Rips stretch
I could be more careful
holding day as if tomorrow
can be contained, netted

don't flirt with buoyancy
the wings blemish to unflight
becoming now unexpected
toddler rock pool smile
jizz and fizzle, released

I recall a hat blown to sea
a lizard skin bones inside out
bright of shine
arch less footsteps parasols
cuttle fish, thousands

a different coast now
every grain nebula
each shore a familiar task
I confess to a dislike of Mahler
hooded plovers bobble, unsupervised

the conservation trench contours
behind shipwreck iron
these little hopes noisy shade
a tidal creek brandishes chromatics
sunburn blusher, 50+

wingnutted Ranga first to go
now more wholemeal in seaweed
a guideline of reef
decades pattern sand blasted cadence
in sight, myself

Slim Pickings

I know the fox's eye
how it carries a tolling
silent there in shadow
alert to my scratching
occasionally periscope up
chary of a final surprise
turning over this for that
all feathers being questions

slow the express

remember Ramon
how we laughed at the delirium
of the pokey seat in the lane
after the readings at La Mama

a promise is a wading thing
and we held a hand each

when you made me write
all seven days to week a month
that stretch of gluten by a wonky light
the way words fall to combine

a separate secret of glow worms
or a far village window by window

I said no man you're better than me
you hugged my wafting shoulder
invited me to the drinks
but the last train stalled us there

in the slipstream between friendship and life

Snail Mail Cursive

concrete cures forever
I was told by a builder
not in the medicinal sense
but strengthening over time

then a letter caught up with me
on this winter's day
so cold two ducks are on the chimney
billing complaint into the ornate mooring

the words came from before death
of our joke about moths in his wallet
he was too cheap for his shout
and how it really happened that day

at the Duke when one flew out
and we were on the floor laughing
just the carpet between infinity
the underlay of worlds

a vibrato knit of things
hand writing filtered by sand
conversations with an albatross
hanging endings in final saliva

the stamp his last touch
when he reached for us on earth
taking three years to berth
with wings from a tropical butterfly

Southern Entry Leongatha, October

The paddocks have changed.
A praying mantis trellis
of snow peas covers banked soil.
On the other road side,
early silage is wrapped garishly
sited like spilled marbles.
White clover counts in threes,
the sky is coffee grounds.
A Norse thunder hooves its way;
the pickers clasp satchels
their non las lift off and spinnaker.
Rain calls them to shelter,
in utes the station plays Orbison.
Holiday traffic slows to read
the stacked rounds broadcasting,
Farmer Looking For Partner
and Carn Dogs 2022.

Summer has its reasons

A koala walked beside me
while I mowed
stopped when I stopped
looked over and slothed along
when I started again

Two black snakes ahead of me
doing it hard
uphill in the driveway
the gravel clinging
their red bellies dusty

Three eagles counting uplifts
tracked me to the dry creek
played keepings off with magpies
I was singing 'Guantanamera'
when the deer sprang

Four horses came Rapunzel manes
a skylark of herded intensity
back kicked against the day
threw heads to say Look Out
snickered me the hints of change

The ants a scurry in Farsi
spelled what they could remember
of the days before tallied landings
bark falling the cast net of trees
freckles infertile seeds

The skies all opening
an upheld portage of locks
gypsy barges in a silhouette
a symphony of continents
the two-finger whistle

I could never do

Sunday 2009, any day a Sunday

By the time the town hall meeting
is called, they have stopped the fire
at the third green. The wind change
waved in presence back to the lake.

The new town is a suburb returned
to earth, a clay pot of dry river bed
in the gully. Ravens and magpies
compete for air to sing in prolapse.

Seb the Sri Lankan counsellor sits
beside me, his gumboots covered
in cold ash. Back at his property
only some steel veranda posts stand.

He's sobbing as he takes my half
used tatty handkerchief, not from
any sorrow this time. Because his
house cow trotted out of the cinders.

Squirting her demands there as he
sat between geography. His family
is safe and there are no casualties,
this time we are boats for salvage.

Surprised bravo by dawn

A rabbit sang outside my window
of the high plains
now chocolate with resowing
at first I thought this not possible
(the rabbit singing I mean)

but a rusty kettle will still boil
even while leaking
the jarrah bench top bronzing
unbuckled by non solar warmth
(the panes broken anyway)

motionless as a captive Durer etching
every muscle outlined
each hair an unruffled mystery
of scattered natural inbreeding
(the myxo eye a little off putting)

a song of ancient lands divided
of travels and pursuit
the piping squealing rising alone
into a wondering day edged open
(the moon in a sirsee falling)

breaking kindling into warmth
misty valley stirring
words failed for timely response
the chance missed for encore
(quiet as the space between pulses)

Swan

For if I die tonight
I've seen the grace in descent
a conclave of souls in mirth
giggling beneath a gravity of feathers
at the sudden embracing stillness
its impossible conclusion in symmetry
leans back holding trapped air posed
touchdown to the surface mirrored
gliding in most gentle repose

That wouldn't work with long division

you get seven with six she reminds me
the young mother who went to school
with my son here where the soil
seems so rich it has forgotten to heal
and I am lost not understanding
stuck without the mercy of silence
it's like a South Australian dozen
she says or half of twelve plus one
I tell her of how my friends
put me up for a night and I stayed for a decade
back in the car I count the extra stubby
that wouldn't work with long division

The trouble with my enemy

His heart inside a large Vegemite jar
held dark viscous in state
salty as a collection basin

Those omnibus tears
rattle against the label
if I turn the screw top clockwise

Only a little, only a little at a time

There breaks a sound
a keen of parent reading a story book
an outlet release of infant hands

Then circles alphabets borderless
frayed and shredding pointers
passwords un entire

Only this morning, only for a while

I could not remember breakfast
and left the supermarket unpaying
the staff were kind

But there's the sun half in the Indian Ocean
a wild west decline in a fire alight
toddler arms and sobbing at my neck

As though the grazed knees might never heal

An anti-turn, and anti-click slow ambience of return
the fuzz of jack in the box memory
caught between the edges hauls out its tongue

Every thing and not a thing
sticking exiting gravel
all placed in set and beaking about underneath

Gliding unready, gliding unready out of swan song

Theatre Road at Dusk

there is a vacancy in my house
that cannot be occupied

an emptiness
lost to deer by fading

headlights are her weakness

an urge to perform
a hand painting given rainbow air

the schooled leap of cosine dance
one precise bound only

across dizzy evening margins

where the vacancy in my house
cannot give audience to an elegance

four becomes one momentarily
in a Fonteyn of grace

she vanishes off stage

as night sways
like a bead curtain

after someone has stepped through

that problem with genuflection

from beneath the widow maker
I rescue the wandered calf
hoisted to my chest it squirms

then settles as a down pillow

perhaps it just dreamed of the view
where the valley achingly redemptive
torques beyond language

amid the dialects of birds

and my seeing
too poor here among the haunches
of a human's roaming salvage

only notices the mother move

as the skinny legs spraddle
its dance to stand and suckle

her glutinous tongue at my lick

a small share of birthing gone
in the time it takes for penance

There's a mystery kid

in some family photos
he's all big eyes red cheeks
and an oversized cardigan
out of place snow in summer
a hair strand on your mouth
not irritating but there

I think his name was Johnny
he's as Catholic as his knees
with a rally in his pose
my sisters are holding me
between them my bended legs
like a chimpanzee wrestling

squirming shy to get away
from that pumped up Santa
garden gnome on steroids
my dummy looks like
it's been dropped a few times
and I don't like clowns
Johnny bit fat Christmas
on his stubby good will hand
a Celtic arc through detente

winked at me getting down
wave of fringe sweeping
a straw cleaning broom
the next picture's blurry
I'm all giddly goo smiles
free on the orphan's tab

They don't know about horses

those who talk of standing sleep
how they curl like cats
snuffle ground as wingless dragons

or idle attent in the full sun

because there are not enough days
to feel earth undulate in the tease of burlap

pose rump into the weather

always alert for the summons
the startled flap of plovers
as unshod hooves cherish gallop

then call across fences

their voices tuned for a herd
whickering out the lost posse

rubbing morse on iron gates

the criss-cross code of a sudden lick
a scrape of brisket colour
to mark the strain in barbed wire

and always their eyes of finest glaze
seeking truth in the most human places

Three hundred and sixty seconds is all it took

fewer than a ghost town
where the currawongs
scrawl their names

the half tail feral cat
hiccups the last budgie's feathers

the post office doors
open outward

once a river dawdled
many places to go

environmental flows
lapsed in occupation
big trees rolled
throughout the compass

six-minute people
scratch out lives
the win beneath the crinkle

hesitates for bearing

set and dawn
the twenty-four hours persist
faith swings
out of the pendulum chime

calls out the broken testament
see what time it really is
against the oldest occupation*

* Indigenous leaders point out that white occupancy of the
Australian continent if measured against the timescale of indigenous
settlement, would amount to only six minutes against 24 hours.

Thy la cine

ce qui aurail pu etre regret pour le plat tigre plate

there's talk they could bring you back
science needs forgiveness
like the rest of us
hind stripes the board
to their noughts and crosses
wipe the chalk off

careful little friend
resurrection in genes
may lose your husky tones
flat jawlines no longer fashionable
those teeth still too sharp
need a little refinement

stay behind the scenes of astronomy in theatre
wave the air between the look
up and down at the hint in glimpse
filtered rainbow along your spine
old films have shadows
that make regret pungent

Triangulation

Between
hospital
cemetery
and rubbish tip
find me in clamour
I have called down swans
a saltpetre of full netting
let swing a while longer
the cardiology spinnaker all squelch
spine as low as the watermark
I remain ungraded
Sift
letters
words
and Carats
find me in pages
I have swum outside flags
a recidivist of book cases
let be the moonstruck owl
the nights unarranged loose chronology
sentences are all hard labour
We remain ungraded

Twelve megawatts to evening

a fox so cruel

in its beautiful unmercy
where black swans

trawl beyond mine shaft warnings

a mob of grey roos
languid as a marinade

scratch at rear thighs

old gardeners resting
on a cushioning rake

the wind turbines

obelisks in need of a pharaoh
sift the sky for a language

only written in stone

at the end of the trail
all this thirsting water

the hospital air ambulance

skims a stitching reverberation
on the midwinter tide

this is a place to lie down

between shaking centuries
let something run away with me

into a chiaroscuro frame

Uncaged animals

They speak
but then they don't
these handlers of truth

their baton tongues rattle
along loose evaporating bars

we see through a decline
without any nurture
the promise withering within

still

I'll hold your hand
step out Fred and Ginger
fall and rise

hand on cuff less wrist
over this diapason rescue

but then again

the sideshow ennui
calls us back
one last performance

we will grow tired
of the ringmaster's whip
stand up with the big cat
nine tails or lives

if you slip
I will slip too
one for one
this is how a number grows.

Unshredded Banksy

The only milk bar left
is up Dairy Lane
on the hill in the Catholic side
where the gravel road
runs beneath flowering grass trees
their creamy spikes
sway a cartoon hula
they made a footpath
at Wishart Street
but only a few metres long
people wrote in it before setting
things like
Johnno, dog paws, ring this number for sex,
even an old Foo.
By the culvert in the dip
the caviar piles of yabbies
speak of other things
like the dark in chocolate
the smell of a barbecue
and how the best moments
are always falling
where the years
just step aside.

Wake of trust

out of this flimsy unbright morning
the sea and highway traffic combine
I am trying my fingers on slowly
to catch a sound of words between

the break of ocean and mechanics
one click for me and one for waking
my shoulders alive from vaccination
a north wind calls down the alps

brings a chill beyond remonstrance
the library fire is meekly alight
a disdain of cat awaits impatient
the shelves page into day blinking

each author stirs again by surname
do they watch for the warm of hope
the gentle alphabet of ease to flame
contained to glassy generations so

we stretch out to catch this comfort
fondled as it is by nuanced arrival
each species drawn to silence for now
a pause beneath each breath of company

Wanna see me juggle

an immeasurable weight
the teardrop falls
everything there is

the anticipation
patting a dog
a travel between lick or bite

fifty years ago I bought the album
with the song of the age I'll be
this summer Christmas

working on my headstone
an abstract of heart on a sleeve
history is truancy

but when my grandfather
was laid out by nanna
in his one occasion suit

she grabbed my wrist laughing
don't lick knives you'll lose a tongue

my uncle that wake
chased us through the house

every room a chatelaine

put us in a hessian bag
an odour of dead fox and ragwort

then we sang battle hymn of the marines
a pianola with woozy recipes
all made of knobbly knees

run rabbit run rabbit run run run

Year without television

our heartbeat slowed
        to the voices of radio
the dog,
head angled ears tuned in
watched,
licked at sound
there was dawdle in step
morning cracked its egg
books and toast
gave over day
we worked that paddock clean
until evening called us in
        to each page-turner
a remit dangling there
left by sightless patience
thinking how each character
spoke without vision
of our remorse into night
no stations for switch
the epilogue bated
asleep shoulder to shoulder

Acknowledgements

Many of these poems, sometimes in a slightly different version,
have appeared in:
Bluepepper
Outlaw Poetry
Your One Phone Call
Silver Birch Press
Somnia.blue
The Blue Nib
StylusLit
Gargouille
The Blog 365+ Project
The Age
The Sydney Morning Herald
SurVision Magazine
Live Encounters Poetry and Writing
Poetica Review
Zoomorphic Magazine
Post – Revue
Ascent Aspirations Magazine
Blank Rune Books Small Press
Impspired Magazine
Nine Muses Poetry
Have Your Chill
Circulo de Poesia
Voice and Verse Poetry Magazine
Punk Noir Magazine
Armagan Literary Magazine
Spare Change News, Cambridge, MA.
Lethe Literary and Art Journal
Grieve Anthology
Uncharted Constellations Anthology
Burrow

About the Author

James Walton is published in many anthologies, journals and newspapers. He has been shortlisted for the ACU National Literature Prize, the MPU International Prize, The William Wantling Prize, the James Tate Prize, The Ada Cambridge Prize, and is a winner of the Raw Art Review Chapbook Competition.

His work is published in many countries, and has been translated into Spanish and Farsi.

He was a librarian, a farm worker, and mostly a public sector union official.

This is his fifth full-length collection.

CPSIA information can be obtained
at www.ICGtesting.com
Printed in the USA
LVHW030222020223
738489LV00013B/967

9 781761 094651